# Just, Speedy, and Inexpensive? An Evaluation of Judicial Case Management Under the Civil Justice Reform Act

James S. Kakalik

Terence Dunworth

Laural A. Hill

Daniel McCaffrey

Marian Oshiro

Nicholas M. Pace

Mary E. Vaiana

RAND

*The Institute for Civil Justice*

## THE INSTITUTE FOR CIVIL JUSTICE

The mission of the Institute for Civil Justice is to help make the civil justice system more efficient and more equitable by supplying policymakers and the public with the results of objective, empirically based, analytic research. The ICJ facilitates change in the civil justice system by analyzing trends and outcomes, identifying and evaluating policy options, and bringing together representatives of different interests to debate alternative solutions to policy problems. The Institute builds on a long tradition of RAND research characterized by an interdisciplinary, empirical approach to public policy issues and rigorous standards of quality, objectivity, and independence.

ICJ research is supported by pooled grants from corporations, trade and professional associations, and individuals; by government grants and contracts; and by private foundations. The Institute disseminates its work widely to the legal, business, and research communities, and to the general public. In accordance with RAND policy, all Institute research products are subject to peer review before publication. ICJ publications do not necessarily reflect the opinions or policies of the research sponsors or of the ICJ Board of Overseers.

# BOARD OF OVERSEERS

# PREFACE

This executive summary summarizes three technical reports that document RAND's evaluation of the Civil Justice Reform Act (CJRA) of 1990. It provides an overview of the purpose of the CJRA, the basic design of the evaluation, the key findings, and their policy implications. It was prepared for the Judicial Conference of the United States.

The three summarized reports are:

> *Implementation of the Civil Justice Reform Act in Pilot and Comparison Districts*, RAND, MR-801-ICJ, by James S. Kakalik, Terence Dunworth, Laural A. Hill, Daniel McCaffrey, Marian Oshiro, Nicholas M. Pace, and Mary E. Vaiana, 1996. This document traces the stages in the implementation of the CJRA in the study districts: the recommendations of the advisory groups, the plans adopted by the districts, and the plans actually implemented.

> *An Evaluation of Judicial Case Management Under the Civil Justice Reform Act*, RAND, MR-802-ICJ, by James S. Kakalik, Terence Dunworth, Laural A. Hill, Daniel McCaffrey, Marian Oshiro, Nicholas M. Pace, and Mary E. Vaiana, 1996. This document presents the main descriptive and statistical evaluation of how the CJRA case management principles implemented in the study districts affected cost, time to disposition, and participants' satisfaction and views of fairness.

> *An Evaluation of Mediation and Early Neutral Evaluation Under the Civil Justice Reform Act*, RAND, MR-803-ICJ, by James S. Kakalik, Terence Dunworth, Laural A. Hill, Daniel McCaffrey, Marian Oshiro, Nicholas M. Pace, and Mary E. Vaiana, 1996. This document discusses the results of an evaluation of mediation and neutral evaluation designed to supplement the alternative dispute resolution assessment contained in the main CJRA evaluation.

For more information about the Institute for Civil Justice contact:

Dr. Deborah Hensler, Director
Institute for Civil Justice
RAND
1700 Main Street, P. O. Box 2138
Santa Monica, CA 90407-2138
TEL: (310) 451-6916
FAX: (310) 451-6979
Internet: Deborah_Hensler@rand.org

A profile of the Institute for Civil Justice, abstracts of its publications, and ordering information can be found on RAND's home page on the World Wide Web at http://www.rand.org/centers/icj/.

# CONTENTS

# ACKNOWLEDGMENTS

We greatly appreciate the cooperation we have received from the Judicial Conference Committee on Court Administration and Case Management; from the Administrative Office of the United States Courts; from the Federal Judicial Center; and from the judges, clerks, advisory group members, and attorneys in the 20 pilot and comparison district courts. Without their cooperation and assistance, this study would not have been possible.

We are also indebted to the thousands of attorneys and litigants who responded to our surveys. They contributed a wealth of information that previously has not been available on litigation time, lawyer hours, litigation costs, satisfaction with the court's management, and views on fairness.

Many people at RAND contributed to this five-year effort. Deborah Hensler, Director of RAND's Institute for Civil Justice, provided sound advice and strong support throughout the study. Dr. Hensler was technical advisor to the Brookings task force. RAND's Survey Research Group conducted our surveys and coded more than 10,000 case dockets under the direction of Laural Hill; we especially thank Eva Feldman, Jo Levy, Don Solosan, and Tim Vernier for their extraordinary efforts and care. Data file design and analyses were conducted under the direction of Marian Oshiro, with timely assistance from Lori Parker and Deborah Wesley. We also are very grateful to Stephen B. Middlebrook, who prepared much of the material on the advisory group process; this work was done in conjunction with his role as a Visiting Fellow with RAND's Institute for Civil Justice in 1994. Mr. Middlebrook was a member of the Brookings task force. Beth Benjamin helped to prepare the chapter on implementation of change in the court system. The insightful comments of RAND reviewers John Adams, Lloyd Dixon, and Peter Jacobson significantly improved the final report. Stephen B. Burbank, Paul D. Carrington, Robert S. Peck, Judith Resnik, Bill Wagner, and H. Thomas Wells, Jr., provided independent outside reviews and many useful comments on drafts of our report. We received excellent secretarial support from Rosa Morinaka and Sharon Welz, especially in dealing with calls from survey recipients. Finally, we appreciate the expert assistance of Patricia Bedrosian, who edited and oversaw production of the final version of this document.

# 1. INTRODUCTION

The Civil Justice Reform Act (CJRA) of 1990 is rooted in more than a decade of concern that cases in federal courts take too long and cost litigants too much. As a consequence, proponents of reform argue, some litigants are denied access to justice and many litigants incur inappropriate burdens when they turn to the courts for assistance in resolving disputes. In the late 1980s, several groups, including the Federal Courts Study Committee and the Council on Competitiveness, began formulating reform proposals. One of these—the Task Force on Civil Justice Reform, which was initiated by Senator Joseph Biden and convened by The Brookings Institution—produced a set of recommendations that ultimately led to legislation. The task force comprised leading litigators from the plaintiffs' and defense bar, civil and women's rights lawyers, attorneys representing consumer and environmental organizations, representatives of the insurance industry, general counsels of major corporations, former judges, and law professors.

*The Civil Justice Reform Act required federal courts to develop plans for reducing cost and delay.*

The new legislation, the CJRA, required each federal district court to conduct a self-study with the aid of an advisory group and to develop a plan for civil case management to reduce costs and delay. To provide an empirical basis for assessing new procedures adopted under the act, the legislation also provided for an independent evaluation. Ten district courts, denoted "pilot" district courts, were required to adopt plans that incorporated certain case management principles through December 1995. The evaluation focused on the consequences of that pilot program.

*The act also mandated an independent evaluation.*

The Judicial Conference and the Administrative Office of the U.S. Courts asked RAND's Institute for Civil Justice to evaluate the implementation and the effects of the CJRA in these districts. This document describes the implementation of the CJRA and summarizes the effects of its case management policies on time to disposition, costs, and participants' satisfaction and views of fairness.

To preview the main findings of the evaluation:

1. The CJRA pilot program, as the package was implemented, had little effect on time to disposition, litigation costs, and attorneys' satisfaction and views of the fairness of case management.

2. But our analysis of case management as practiced across districts and judges shows that what judges do to manage cases matters:

   - Early judicial case management, setting the trial schedule early, shortened time to discovery cutoff, and having litigants at or available for settlement conferences are associated with a significantly reduced time to disposition. Early judicial case management also is associated with significantly increased costs to litigants, as measured by attorney work hours.

- Shortened time to discovery cutoff is associated with significantly decreased attorney work hours.

- None of these policies significantly affects attorneys' satisfaction or views of fairness, either positively or negatively.

3. If early case management and early setting of the trial schedule are combined with shortened discovery cutoff, the increase in costs associated with the former can be offset by the decrease in costs associated with the latter. We estimate that under these circumstances, litigants in general civil cases that do not close within the first nine months would pay no cost penalty for a reduced time to disposition of approximately four to five months (about 30 percent of their median time to disposition).

4. The CJRA also required public reporting of the status of each judge's calendar every six months, including the number of cases pending over three years. Since adoption of the CJRA, the total number of all civil cases pending has increased, but the number of cases pending more than three years has dropped by about 25 percent from its pre-CJRA level.

## 2. OVERVIEW OF THE CJRA PILOT PROGRAM

The CJRA created a pilot program that required ten federal district courts to incorporate certain case management principles into their plans and to consider incorporating certain other case management techniques. Both the principles and the techniques were largely based on those recommended by the task force initiated by Senator Biden. The evaluation included ten other districts to permit comparisons; these districts were not required to adopt any of the case management principles or techniques.

*A key element in the CJRA evaluation was a pilot program.*

The ten pilot districts selected by the Committee on Court Administration and Case Management of the Judicial Conference of the United States were: California (S), Delaware, Georgia (N), New York (S), Oklahoma (W), Pennsylvania (E), Tennessee (W), Texas (S), Utah, and Wisconsin (E).

The Judicial Conference, with advice from RAND, also selected the following ten comparison districts: Arizona, California (C), Florida (N), Illinois (N), Indiana (N), Kentucky (E), Kentucky (W), Maryland, New York (E), and Pennsylvania (M).

Using several methods, we confirmed that the pilot and comparison districts are comparable and adequately represent the range of districts in the United States. Together, the 20 study districts have about one-third of all federal judges and one-third of all federal case filings.

The pilot districts were required to implement their plans by January 1992; the other 84 districts, including the comparison districts, could implement their plans any time before December 1993.

### THE SIX CASE MANAGEMENT PRINCIPLES

The act directs each pilot district to incorporate the following principles into its plan:

*Ten pilot districts were required to adopt six case management principles.*

1. Differential case management;

2. Early judicial management;

3. Monitoring and control of complex cases;

4. Encouragement of cost-effective discovery through voluntary exchanges and cooperative discovery devices;

5. Good-faith efforts to resolve discovery disputes before filing motions; and

6. Referral of appropriate cases to alternative dispute resolution programs.

Pilot districts *must* incorporate these principles, while other districts *may* do so.

## THE SIX CASE MANAGEMENT TECHNIQUES

*Districts also had to consider adopting certain other techniques.*

The act directs each district to *consider* incorporating the following techniques into its plan, but no district is *required* to incorporate them:

1. Joint discovery/case management plan;

2. Party representation at each pretrial conference by an attorney with authority to bind that party regarding all matters previously identified by the court for discussion at the conference;

3. Required signature of attorney and party on all requests for discovery extensions or trial postponements;

4. Early neutral evaluation;

5. Party representatives with authority to bind to be present or available by telephone at settlement conferences; and

6. Other features that the court considers appropriate.

## 3. FEATURES OF THE RAND EVALUATION

The evaluation is designed to provide a quantitative and qualitative basis for assessing how the case management principles and techniques identified in the CJRA affect litigants' costs (measured in both attorney work hours and money), time to disposition, participants' satisfaction with the process, views of fairness of the process, and judge work time required.

*The evaluation assesses the effects of case management on time, cost, satisfaction, and views of fairness.*

Comparisons are made between the ten pilot and ten comparison districts using data from cases terminated in 1991 before CJRA and separately using data from cases filed in 1992–93 after implementation of the pilot program plans. Because of differences between our pre-CJRA and post-CJRA data that are unrelated to CJRA and that are difficult to properly account for, we focus on separate pre- and post-CJRA analyses. The results of our qualitative analysis, combined with our separate pre- and post-CJRA quantitative analyses, provide ample evidence concerning the effects of the act.

The evaluation also uses quantitative analyses to compare cases managed in different ways to determine how such management practices affect litigants' costs, time to disposition, participants' satisfaction with the process, and views of fairness. The quantitative analyses exploit natural variation in judges' management practices, rather than an experimental random assignment of management practices to cases.

### DATA SOURCES

The evaluation is based on extensive and detailed case-level data from January 1991 through December 1995. Data sources include:

- Court records;
- Records, reports, and surveys of CJRA advisory groups;
- The districts' cost and delay reduction plans;
- Detailed case processing and docket information on a sample of cases;
- Surveys of judicial officers on their activities, time expenditures, and views of CJRA;
- Mail surveys of attorneys and litigants about costs, time, satisfaction, and views of the fairness of the process; and
- Interviews in person with judges, court staff, and lawyers in each of the 20 districts.

happened as a result of CJRA and the application of management principles and techniques identified in the act; we leave it to others to draw conclusions on the issue of uniformity of rules and procedures.

## 4. OVERVIEW OF THE CJRA's IMPLEMENTATION

### THE ADVISORY GROUP PROCESS

The CJRA empowered some 2,000 people across the country to examine, diagnose, and prescribe remedies for the federal civil justice system. These individuals were organized into advisory groups in each of the 94 districts.

The groups' mandate was to assess the condition of the civil and criminal dockets, identify the principal causes of delay and excess cost, and make recommendations, which the court was free to accept or reject, for dealing with these problems. The advisory groups were also to monitor the implementation of the plan and provide input to an annual reassessment for each district.

The act calls for a "balanced" composition of the advisory group, to include not only attorneys but also other persons who can speak for major categories of litigants. That balance was met for the vast majority of the advisory groups as far as lawyers are concerned. "Other persons" were minimally represented. Limited by their lack of familiarity with the federal district court system, lay people usually played only a very modest role in meetings of the advisory groups.

In general, the advisory groups approached their mission with dedication and conscientiousness. They analyzed the data that courts already had regarding time to disposition, but they had little information on litigation costs with which to work. Many groups supplemented court data with interviews of judges and court clerks and with surveys of attorneys and, occasionally, litigants. The advisory groups' final reports reflected considerable independence from the courts. Most courts incorporated most of their advisory group's recommendations into their plans.

Our interviews and the available documents suggest that the quality of the required annual reassessments varies markedly from district to district. Although the act does not require a written assessment, seven of the 20 districts in this study have done written reassessments at least twice. Six of the 20 districts had no written documentation of the results of any annual assessment when we inquired in January 1996.

Our interviews indicate that generating the reports and plans required by the act have made district courts more cognizant of case management problems and opportunities. Bench-bar understanding reportedly has also been improved. That benefit alone probably justifies the advisory groups' work.

*Advisory groups played a key role in developing each district's case management plan.*

*Most advisory group members were lawyers.*

*Most courts adopted their advisory group's recommendations.*

*Factors beyond the courts' control may influence cost and delay.*

Several of the CJRA advisory group assessments contended that certain factors beyond the courts' direct control influence civil litigation cost and delay. Three factors predominated: First, the assessments cited the pressure generated by the criminal docket. Legislation creating new federal crimes, adoption of the Speedy Trial Act, and the advent of mandatory sentencing guidelines all increase the burden on the federal court and provide less time for the orderly movement of civil cases. Second, the assessments noted that judicial vacancies are being left unfilled for substantial periods of time. Third, the need for better assessment of the effect of proposed legislation on the courts' workload was highlighted.

## NATURE OF THE CJRA PLANS

*All pilot districts complied with the act's statutory language...*

All pilot districts complied with the statutory language in the act, which provides loosely defined principles but leaves operational interpretation to the discretion of individual districts and judicial officers.

*...but the amount of change varied widely.*

Many pilot and comparison districts interpreted some or all of their current and past practices to be consistent with the language of the act and continued those practices unchanged. However, if the spirit of the act is interpreted to mean experimentation and change focusing on the six CJRA principles, then the pilot districts met that spirit to varying degrees.

Comparison districts, having no mandated policies, generally made fewer changes than pilot districts.

*In some districts, planned changes were not fully implemented.*

Even in pilot districts whose plans suggested major changes, implementation often fell short. Thus, there was less change in case management after CJRA than one might have expected from reading the plans.

However, implementing the pilot plans may have heightened the consciousness of judges and lawyers and brought about some important implicit shifts in attitude and approach to case management on the part of the bench and bar. For example, our interviews suggested, and the case-level data we collected confirmed, that the fraction of cases managed early has increased and that time to discovery cutoff has shortened.

## 5. IMPLEMENTATION AND EFFECTS OF THE CJRA CASE MANAGEMENT POLICIES

The six principles and six techniques specified in the act can be usefully assigned to four categories: differential case management, early judicial management, discovery management, and alternative dispute resolution. We use these categories in our discussion of how the CJRA's case management principles were implemented in the 20 study districts and how these policies affected time to disposition, costs, satisfaction, and views of fairness.

The evaluation presented in this chapter is based on quantitative analyses that compare cases managed in different ways to determine the effects of different management practices. These analyses exploit observational data resulting from the naturally occurring variation in judges' management practices, rather than data from an experimental random assignment of management practices to cases. These observational data have certain inherent constraints. In particular, judges and districts choose to use certain case management policies and practices, and we must assume that these judges and districts could differ from other judges and districts choosing not to use them. Because of these potential differences, our observed effects of a particular case management practice should be treated as an upper bound to what might occur if other judges and districts were asked to implement that practice.

### DIFFERENTIAL CASE MANAGEMENT

The essence of the differential case management (DCM) concept is that different types of cases need different types and levels of judicial management. One way to implement DCM is to create a number of separate *tracks*, each of which implies a prescribed structured approach to case scheduling and management, and to assign cases early to these tracks. The traditional approach is the *judicial discretion* model, in which judges make management decisions for general civil cases case by case.

*Tracks and judicial discretion are two approaches to differential case management.*

#### Implementation

Before CJRA, all courts had special management procedures for "minimal management" cases such as prisoner petitions other than death penalty cases, Social Security appeals, government loan recovery, and bankruptcy appeals. After CJRA, all courts retained their procedures for these cases with little modification.

Minimal management cases are typically disposed of relatively quickly and cheaply with little or no judicial management necessary. Since districts made few changes in their procedures for minimal management types of cases, and since almost none of these cases are managed using the policies and procedures that apply to general civil litigation and that are the focus of the CJRA, they could not inform our evaluation of the procedures of concern in the CJRA. For all of these reasons, we exclude the category of minimal management cases from our statistical analyses.

*We cannot evaluate the effects of the track approach because only one pilot district implemented it with sufficient volume.*

Before CJRA, the predominant approach to case management in all 20 study districts was the judicial discretion model. Six of the ten pilot districts planned to replace this model with a track model, but that model proved difficult to implement. Most districts that included tracking in their plan actually assigned the traditional group of minimal management case types to an expedited track. Five of the six pilot districts whose plans contained a track model assigned 2 percent or less of their cases to the complex track. The consequence was that almost all general civil cases to which CJRA procedural principles might be relevant were placed in the standard track, if any track assignment was made. This meant that there was little actual "differential" tracking of general civil cases in most districts that adopted a track model in their CJRA plan.

Only the Pennsylvania (E) pilot district implemented its tracks for all general civil cases and had over 2 percent of the cases assigned to the complex track. That district also implemented other changes, the results of which we cannot reliably separate from the effects of the track system. Consequently, we have no basis for evaluating how the track method of DCM affected time, cost, satisfaction, and views of fairness.

Interviews with judges and lawyers suggest some reasons for the lack of experimentation with and successful implementation of a tracking system of DCM for general civil litigation. They include (1) the difficulty in determining the correct track assignment for most civil litigation cases using data available at or soon after case filing; and (2) judges' desire to tailor case management to the needs of the case and to their style of management rather than having the track assignment provide the management structure for a category of cases.

With respect to the difficulty in determining the correct track assignment for a case, our statistical analysis indicates that the objective data available at the time of filing (such as nature of suit category, origin, jurisdiction, and number of parties) are not particularly good predictors of either time to disposition or cost of litigation. This suggests that, if a track model is to be implemented, decisions about track assignments should be supplemented with subjective information from the lawyers or judge.

Special management of complex cases, the third CJRA principle, is a subset of differential case management. This principle lacked an implementation sufficiently consistent and well documented to permit evaluation. These cases are generally managed individually by the judge.

## EARLY JUDICIAL MANAGEMENT

Early judicial case management includes the CJRA principle of early and ongoing judicial control of pretrial processes as well as the optional CJRA technique of having counsel jointly present a discovery/case management plan at the initial pretrial conference. Related CJRA techniques include: parties being represented at pretrial conferences by an attorney with authority to bind them; requiring the signature of the attorney and the party on all requests for discovery extensions or postponements of trial; and requiring party representatives with authority to bind to be present or available by telephone at settlement conferences.

### Implementation

All advisory group reports favored the principle of early judicial management of general civil cases, and all of the courts' plans accepted the principle of early and ongoing judicial control of the pretrial process. However, case management styles varied considerably between districts and between judges in a given district.

*In practice, early judicial management varied between districts and judges.*

Implementation of the four suggested techniques in this area varied substantially. Before CJRA, only one district in our study required that counsel jointly present a discovery/case management plan at the initial pretrial conference, although at least one other district required the attorneys to confer before the first pretrial conference to attempt to agree on a scheduling order. Four of the ten pilot districts adopted this technique in their plans, and nine of the other pilot and comparison districts later adopted it after our sample cases were selected when the December 1993 federal rules changes were made.

*Implementation of the CJRA techniques also varied.*

Both before and after CJRA, all 20 districts required or allowed judges to require that each party be represented at each pretrial conference by an attorney with authority to bind that party. Since there was no variation in policies between districts, we could not evaluate this technique.

In contrast, both before and after CJRA, none of the 20 districts required the signature of the attorney and the party on all requests for discovery extensions or postponements of trial.

Finally, before CJRA, eight of the 20 districts required, upon notice by the court, that party representatives with authority to bind be present or available by telephone at settlement conferences. Five additional districts adopted this technique as part of their CJRA plan.

## Effects

*Early judicial management significantly reduces time to disposition—but increases litigation costs.*

In our statistical analyses, we defined early judicial case management as any schedule, conference, status report, joint plan, or referral to ADR within 180 days of case filing. This definition gives time for nearly all cases to have service and answer or other appearance of the defendants (which legally can take up to six months), so issue is joined, and it is appropriate to begin management if the judge wants to do so.

Early judicial case management has significant effects on both time and cost. We estimate a 1.5 to 2 month reduction in median time to disposition for cases that last at least nine months, and an approximately 20-hour increase in lawyer work hours. Our data show that the costs to litigants are also higher in dollar terms and in litigant hours spent when cases are managed early. These results debunk the myth that reducing time to disposition will necessarily reduce litigation costs.

Lawyer work hours may increase as a result of early management because lawyers need to respond to a court's management—for example, talking to the litigant and to the other lawyers in advance of a conference with the judge, traveling, and spending time waiting at the courthouse, meeting with the judge, and updating the file after the conference. In addition, once judicial case management has begun, a discovery cutoff date has usually been established, and attorneys may feel an obligation to begin discovery. Doing so could shorten time to disposition, but it may also increase lawyer work hours on cases that were about to settle when the judge began early management.

Early management has no significant effect on lawyer satisfaction or views on fairness. Litigant data showed mixed results for satisfaction with early management, higher in the pre-CJRA sample and lower in the post-CJRA sample.

We also explored alternative definitions of "early" using time periods other than six months, with results similar to those reported here. This finding suggests that the *fact* of management adds to the lawyer work hours, not the "earliness" of the management. However, starting earlier than six months means that more cases would be managed because more cases are still open, so more cases would incur the predicted increase in lawyer work hours. Early management involves a tradeoff between shortened time to disposition and increased lawyer work hours.

*Including early setting of a trial date as part of early management reduces time further.*

In terms of predicting reduced time to disposition, setting a schedule for trial early was the most important component of early management. Including early setting of trial date as part of the early management package yields an additional reduction of 1.5 to 2 months in estimated time to disposition but no further significant change in lawyer work hours.

No other aspect of early judicial management had a consistently significant effect on time to disposition, costs, or attorneys' satisfaction or views of fairness.

Figures 1 and 2 graphically illustrate the effects of early judicial management and early schedule for trial on time to disposition for the cases in the 1992–93 sample. In Figure 1, the "not early" line is higher than the "early" line for the first six months because the former category includes cases that close almost immediately, before the judge has a chance to manage them.

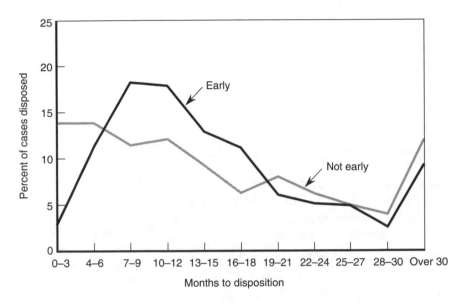

**Figure 1—Effects of Early Judicial Management on Time to Disposition: 1992–93 General Civil Cases with Issue Joined**

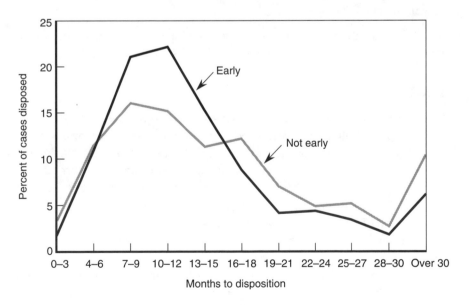

**Figure 2—Effects of Early Schedule for Trial on Time to Disposition: 1992–93 General Civil Cases with Issue Joined**

The technique of having litigants at or available for settlement conferences is associated with statistically significantly reduced time to disposition. However, it has no significant relationship to attorney work hours or satisfaction and no consistent statistically significant relationship to attorneys' views of fairness.

## DISCOVERY MANAGEMENT

Discovery management policies include the CJRA principles of early and ongoing judicial control of pretrial processes, exchanging information early without formal discovery, and requiring good-faith efforts to resolve discovery disputes before filing motions.

### Implementation

*CJRA had little effect on discovery limitation policy but substantially changed early disclosure.*

Before CJRA, most districts left court control of the volume and timing of discovery to the judge in each case; CJRA had little effect on this arrangement. However, the median district times to discovery cutoff were lowered in some of the study districts. For example, in 1991 the fastest and slowest districts' median days from schedule to discovery cutoff were 100 and 274 days, respectively. In 1992–93, these medians had fallen to 83 and 217 days, respectively.

CJRA brought about substantial change in early disclosure. Only one district required it before CJRA; since CJRA, all pilot and comparison districts adopted one of five approaches providing either voluntary or mandatory exchange of information by lawyers, sometimes only for specified types of cases.

All districts retained or strengthened their existing requirements that lawyers certify good-faith efforts to resolve discovery disputes.

### Effects

*Shorter time to discovery cutoff significantly reduces both time to disposition and costs.*

Shorter time from setting a discovery schedule to discovery cutoff is associated with both significantly reduced time to disposition and significantly reduced lawyer work hours. If a district's median discovery cutoff is reduced from 180 days to 120 days, the estimated median time to disposition falls by about 1.5 months for cases that last at least nine months. In addition, lawyer work hours fall by about 17 hours—about 25 percent of their median work hours. These benefits are achieved without any significant change in attorney satisfaction or views of fairness. The data on costs to litigants in dollar terms and in litigant hours spent appear consistent with the data on lawyer work hours. Litigant data also show little difference in satisfaction between shorter and longer time to discovery cutoff.

Neither mandatory nor voluntary early disclosure significantly affects time or costs. Furthermore, we found that cases from districts with a policy of mandatory disclosure of information bearing on *both* sides of the case did not differ significantly in terms of time to disposition from other cases.

*Early disclosure did not significantly affect time or cost.*

But the type of disclosure influences lawyer satisfaction. Lawyers are significantly less satisfied when a district has a policy of mandatory disclosure. However, they tend to be significantly more satisfied when they actually participate in early disclosure on *their* case.

According to our analysis of dockets on more than 5,000 cases, and according to judges we have interviewed in pilot and comparison districts that implemented their plans in December 1991, motions regarding early mandatory disclosure of information are extremely rare. Despite the dire warnings of critics of early mandatory disclosure, we did not find any explosion of ancillary litigation and motion practice related to disclosure in any of the pilot or comparison districts using mandatory disclosure.

*Early mandatory disclosure did not generate an explosion of ancillary litigation.*

## ALTERNATIVE DISPUTE RESOLUTION

The CJRA's ADR policies include diverting cases, when appropriate, to ADR programs and offering an early neutral evaluation program.

### Implementation

The plans from all 20 districts permit the use of ADR techniques. In implementation, however, two different types of programs have emerged, both of which meet the loosely defined requirements of the CJRA. About half the districts have structured and administratively supported programs that involve from 2 to 19 percent of all cases filed, and one district uses early neutral evaluation conducted by a magistrate judge on 50 percent of its cases. The other districts have unstructured programs that do not generate much activity.

### Effects

The three study districts that used mandatory arbitration before CJRA have continued to do so, and two of the three study districts authorized to use voluntary arbitration have started doing so. However, there has been a marked shift in half of the pilot districts toward other structured and administratively supported ADR programs—especially mandatory or voluntary mediation and early neutral evaluation.

*The use of mediation and neutral evaluation has increased.*

Some districts with structured programs have only 2 to 4 percent of their cases referred to ADR, so structure appears to be a necessary but not sufficient feature for a volume ADR program. However, districts that permit ADR of some kind without a structured and administratively supported program have referred few cases to ADR.

*No major effects of mandatory arbitration were detected.*

Our statistical analyses of cases referred to mandatory arbitration detected no major effect of arbitration on time to disposition, lawyer work hours, or lawyer satisfaction. The findings for views of fairness were inconclusive. However, the small sample of arbitration referrals allows us to detect only major effects, not more modest ones.

*Voluntary ADR of any kind was not used extensively.*

Neither lawyers nor judges have used any type of ADR extensively when its use is voluntary.

Using our main CJRA evaluation sample data, we cannot statistically analyze the effects of the other types of ADR used in pilot and comparison districts. The volume of cases referred to ADR was too small to generate a large enough sample when all cases were sampled at random. And each of the various mediation and neutral evaluation programs was sufficiently different to make pooling the data problematic.

### Supplemental Evaluation of Mediation and Early Neutral Evaluation

To supplement the ADR component of the main CJRA evaluation, we conducted a study of mediation and early neutral evaluation in six districts: California (S), New York (E), New York (S), Pennsylvania (E), Oklahoma (W), and Texas (S). These districts were chosen because they use these ADR techniques for a large enough number of cases to permit meaningful statistical evaluation. As Table 1 shows, the programs vary considerably on a number of dimensions, including whether the program is mandatory or voluntary, the point in the litigation at which referral occurs, the purpose of the program, the length of sessions, the type of provider, and the cost to parties.

*Our study detected no major effects of mediation or early neutral evaluation on time, costs, views of fairness, or attorney satisfaction.*

In most of the districts, the percentage of all case filings in a year referred to mediation or neutral evaluation programs was about 5 percent; in CA(S), 50 percent of all cases were referred to its mandatory neutral evaluation program.

Our evaluation provided no strong statistical evidence that the mediation or neutral evaluation programs as implemented in these districts significantly affected time to disposition, litigation costs, or attorney views of fairness or satisfaction with case management. The low completion rate for our litigant surveys does not allow us to make meaningful statistical inferences from the litigant data.

*Money is more likely to change hands when mediation is involved.*

Our only statistically significant finding is that the mediation programs appear to increase the likelihood of a monetary settlement. A plausible explanation for this pattern is that the mediation process is designed to facilitate settlement and does indeed increase the number of cases that

Table 1

CHARACTERISTICS OF ADR PROGRAMS STUDIED

| District Program | Type of Referral | When Referred | Program Emphasis | Cases Included | Typical Session | ADR Provider | Median Fee |
|---|---|---|---|---|---|---|---|
| Mediation | | | | | | | |
| NY(S) | Mandatory | After management track is assigned | Settlement | Random, experimental design | 5 hours over 2 days | Lawyers | None |
| PA(E) | Mandatory | 90 days from filing | Case issues, settlement | Random, experimental design | Single 90 minute session | Lawyers | None |
| OK(W) | Voluntary; or mandatory at judicial discretion | Initial pretrial conference | Settlement | All cases required to have pretrial conference | Single 4 hour session | Lawyers | $660, split by parties |
| TX(S) | Voluntary, tougher cases encouraged; or mandatory at judicial discretion | Initial pretrial conference or later | Settlement | All cases required to have pretrial conference | Single 8 hour session | Lawyers | $1,800, split by parties |
| Neutral Evaluation | | | | | | | |
| CA(S) | Mandatory | Before initial pretrial conference | Evaluation, settlement | All cases required to have pretrial conference | 2.5 hours over 2 days | Magistrate judges handling pretrial case management | None |
| NY(E) | Mandatory at judicial discretion; or voluntary | Initial pretrial conference or later | Settlement | Any eligible case with value >$100,000 | Single 3.5 hour session | Lawyers | None |

settle rather than being dropped or decided by a judge on the basis of motions. When parties reach an agreement and settle the case, that disposition is likely to involve a monetary outcome.

The total court costs of providing the ADR programs in the districts we studied range from $130 to $490 per case (1995 dollars). PA(E) and TX(S) are at the lower end of this continuum; both districts have relatively high volume and relatively few personnel assigned to the program. At the high end are NY(E) and OK(W); in these districts, there are few personnel assigned but also relatively few referrals. CA(S) and NY(S) have costs per case of about $400. These districts have both a relatively high volume of referrals as well as a number of staff assigned to the program.

*Court costs per case to administer the ADR programs range from $130 to $490.*

Program start-up costs to district courts range from $10,000 to $69,000 (1995 dollars). The difference is driven primarily by whether the advisory group or the court did most of the start-up work and whether the district provided training.

*The timing of the ADR session may affect the probability of settlement.*

Participants in these ADR programs—both lawyers and litigants—are generally supportive of them and view the programs as worthwhile in general as well as valuable to their individual cases. However, this general satisfaction with the process does not mean that participants thought it was perfect. The problem cited most often by lawyers and ADR providers was that the parties were not ready to settle when the ADR session was held. The timing of the ADR session could be a major factor in this lack of "readiness." It may be best to conduct the sessions in an atmosphere where at least the basic facts and positions are known to both sides and to the ADR provider as well. Substantial numbers of lawyers in some districts felt that the sessions were held too early to be useful.

We conclude that the mediation and neutral evaluation programs as implemented in these districts are not a panacea for perceived problems of cost and delay, but neither do they appear to be detrimental. We have no justification for strong policy recommendations because we found no major effects from them, either positive or negative. The finding that ADR has no significant effect on time or cost is generally consistent with the results of prior empirical research on court-related ADR.

## MAGISTRATE JUDGES

The last CJRA technique, "other features," was intended to give districts some latitude in their plans. One case management approach included here is the use of magistrate judges in the civil pretrial process.

*Districts use magistrate judges in various ways.*

Districts vary in the roles assigned to magistrate judges on civil cases. Virtually all districts' magistrate judges conduct felony preliminary proceedings and try misdemeanor and petty offense cases. In some districts, magistrate judges are also given felony pretrial duties, including motions, pretrial conferences, and evidentiary hearings. Prisoner cases are routinely referred to magistrate judges in many districts for pretrial management and the preparation of reports and recommendations.

With respect to other civil cases, magistrate judges conduct almost all civil pretrial proceedings in some courts, preparing the case for trial before the assigned district judge. In other courts, they are assigned duties in non-prisoner civil cases on a selective basis in accordance with the preferences of the assigning district judge. In addition, magistrate judges conduct jury and nonjury trials and dispose of civil cases with the consent of the litigants. In two of our study districts—CA(S) and NY(E)—magistrate judges actively manage all aspects of the pretrial process, and usually make early attempts to settle cases. This style of case management differs markedly from the traditional approach used in most other districts before CJRA.

We found that *increased* magistrate judge activity on civil cases had no significant effect on time to disposition or on lawyer work hours, and no consistently significant effect on attorneys' views of fairness associated with changing the level of magistrate judge activity. This *does not* mean that what magistrate judges *do* to manage cases has no significant effect. We believe that districts with higher levels of magistrate judge activity on civil cases are usually using them to conduct pretrial processing that would otherwise be conducted by a district judge. Hence, we believe our statistical findings mean that using magistrate judges *instead of district judges* to conduct pretrial civil case processing does not significantly affect time to disposition, lawyer work hours, or attorney views of fairness.

In the post-CJRA data, we find that increased magistrate judge activity on civil cases is a strong and statistically significant predictor of greater attorney satisfaction. Our interviews with lawyers suggest they are more satisfied with magistrate judges because they find them more accessible than district judges.

These findings suggest that some magistrate judges may be substituted for district judges on non-dispositive pretrial activities without drawbacks and with an increase in lawyer satisfaction.

*Substituting magistrate judges for district judges to do pretrial case management did not significantly affect time, costs, or attorney views of fairness.*

*Lawyers were significantly more satisfied with magistrate judges, perhaps because lawyers find them more accessible.*

## 6.  EFFECTS OF THE CJRA PILOT PROGRAM AS A PACKAGE

*The CJRA pilot program, as the package was implemented, had little effect on time, costs, or attorneys' satisfaction or views of fairness.*

What was the effect of requiring pilot districts to adopt the package of broadly defined case management principles?

*We conclude that the CJRA pilot program, as the package was implemented, had little effect on time to disposition, costs, or attorneys' satisfaction or views of fairness.*

We based this assessment on statistical analysis of cases in pilot and comparison districts, on the results of judicial time studies, and on our survey of judges about how they managed cases before and after CJRA.

### STATISTICAL ANALYSIS OF CASES IN PILOT AND COMPARISON DISTRICTS

*After CJRA, we found no significant differences between pilot and comparison districts in time, cost, satisfaction, or views of fairness.*

In 1991, before the pilot program was implemented, we detected no significant difference between pilot and comparison district cases in time to disposition, lawyer work hours, satisfaction, or views of fairness.

In 1992–93, after the pilot program was implemented but before eight of the comparison districts had implemented their CJRA plans, we still found no significant difference between pilot and comparison district cases in time to disposition, lawyer work hours, satisfaction, or views of fairness.

Figures 3 and 4 illustrate these findings.

Figure 3 shows median months to disposition and median lawyer work hours.  In neither case was there a statistically significant difference between the pilot and comparison districts.  Figure 4 shows a similar pattern of results for participants' satisfaction and views of fairness.

We believe there are at least four reasons why we did not see a significant difference between pilot and comparison districts after the pilot program was implemented.

- Some pilot districts' plans, as implemented, did not result in any major change in case management.

- Some pilot districts' plans that resulted in major change in management at the case level did not apply that change to a large percentage of cases within the district.

- Some changes that were more widely implemented (such as early mandatory disclosure of information) did not significantly affect time, cost, satisfaction, or views of fairness.

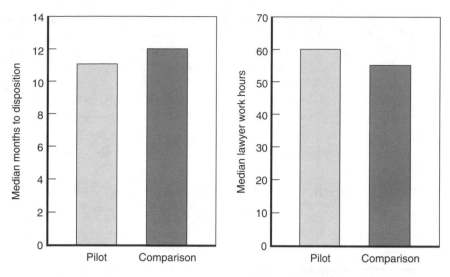

Figure 3—Pilot Program Had No Significant Effects: Time and Cost

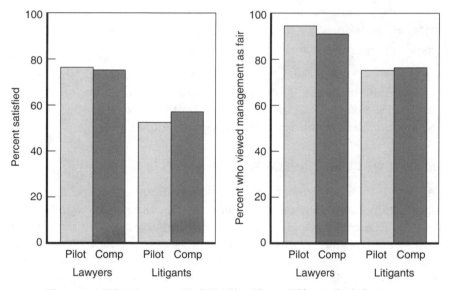

Figure 4—Pilot Program Had No Significant Effects: Satisfaction
and Views of Fairness

• Some case management practices identified as significant predictors of effects are implemented not at the district level, but at the case level, and there is much variation in case management among judges in both the pilot and comparison districts.

## RESULTS OF JUDICIAL TIME STUDY

One concern raised about implementing new case management policies is that benefits such as faster time to disposition may come at the cost of increased time spent by judicial officers. To determine if the judicial case management principles and techniques of the Civil Justice Reform Act

*Judges did not spend more time on civil cases after CJRA . . .*

increased the amount of judicial time spent on civil cases, we conducted a "judicial time study" of time spent on the cases in our samples of 1992–93 civil filings and compared the results with data from the judicial time study conducted by the Federal Judicial Center in the late 1980s.

We found almost no difference in the time spent by judicial officers per civil case in 1992–93 when compared to 1989. The difference in the median time reported per civil case was only one minute; the difference in the mean was six minutes.

## SURVEY OF JUDGES ABOUT CASE MANAGEMENT APPROACH

*. . . and most said they were not managing cases differently.*

In the 1992–93 sample of cases, we surveyed the judge after case closure and received over 3,000 responses. One question concerned the difference in case management before and after CJRA: "Was there a difference in how you and any other judicial officer managed this case, compared to how you would have managed it if it had been disposed of *prior* to January 1, 1992?"

The vast majority of the judges (85 percent in pilot districts, 92 percent in comparison districts) answered "no difference."

Of the 15 percent of the pilot judges who did report a difference, about half said the new case management policies and procedures were better than those before CJRA and about half said they were about the same. None said the new policies were worse than before CJRA.

## EFFECT OF PUBLIC REPORTING?

*Public reports on each judge may have decreased the number of cases pending more than three years.*

Although the pilot program has had no significant effects on time, cost, satisfaction, or views of fairness, there is some evidence that another part of the CJRA may have affected the number of cases pending more than three years in both pilot and comparison districts. The CJRA requires that "The Director of the Administrative Office of the United States Courts shall prepare a semiannual report, available to the public, that discloses for each judicial officer . . . the number and names of cases that have not been terminated within three years after filing." Since public reports on each judge were required, the total number of all civil cases pending has increased, but the number of cases pending more than three years has dropped by about 25 percent from its pre-CJRA level. Nationwide, about 6 percent of all terminations (excluding asbestos cases) are more than three years old. In the pilot and comparison districts, the percentage of terminated cases more than three years old has drifted downward since the passage of the CJRA from 6.8 percent in 1990 to 5.2 percent in 1995 (see Figure 5).

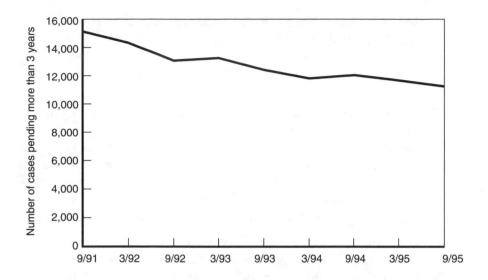

**Figure 5—Public Reports on Each Judge May Have Decreased Number of Cases Pending More Than Three Years**

# 7. IMPLICATIONS FOR A PROMISING CASE MANAGEMENT PACKAGE

*Despite the pilot program's lack of effect, what judges do to manage cases matters.*

The CJRA *pilot program, as the package was implemented,* had little effect on time to disposition, costs, satisfaction, or views of fairness. But this finding does not imply that *case management* has no significant effect. Because case management varies across judges and districts, we were able to assess the effects of specific procedures and techniques on time to disposition, costs, and attorneys' satisfaction and views of fairness. This assessment clearly shows that what judges do to manage cases matters.

Table 2 summarizes the estimated effects of those principles and techniques for which the data permitted evaluation. Those CJRA case management principles that we could not evaluate, because of the way in which the CJRA was implemented, may or may not affect cost and time.

*Case management procedures have a substantial effect on predicted time to disposition.*

**Case management procedures have a substantial predicted effect on time to disposition.** Case management variables accounted for fully half of the explained variance in our analysis of time to disposition.

Four case management procedures showed consistent statistically significant effects on time to disposition: (1) early judicial management; (2) setting the trial schedule early; (3) reducing time to discovery cutoff; and (4) having litigants at or available on the telephone for settlement conferences. For general civil cases with issue joined that do not close within the first nine months, we estimate that these procedures have the *combined effect* of reducing median time to disposition by about four to five months in our post-CJRA sample—about 30 percent of their median time to disposition.

*But procedural reform as specified in the CJRA may have a limited role in reducing litigation costs.*

**In contrast, judicial case management policy appears to have a limited role to play in reducing litigation costs.** Of all the policy and procedure variables we investigated as possible predictors of reduced lawyer work hours, only judicial management of discovery seemed to produce the desired effect. Cases from districts with shorter median discovery cutoff times tend to require fewer lawyer hours; in contrast, cases with early management tended to require more.

Several attorney and case characteristics—especially case stakes and case complexity—explain more of the variance in lawyer work hours than do the case management variables. It appears that lawyer work hours are driven predominantly by factors other than case management. When time to disposition is cut, lawyers seem to do much the same work, but do it in less time.

Table 2

## SUMMARY OF STATISTICAL EVALUATION OF CJRA PRINCIPLES AND TECHNIQUES

| Principle or Technique | Time to Disposition | Cost (Lawyer Work Hours) | Lawyer Satisfaction | Lawyer Perception of Fairness |
|---|---|---|---|---|
| Early judicial management of any type | S − | S + | 0 | 0 |
| Effect of including trial schedule set early as part of early management | S − | 0 | 0 | 0 |
| Effect of including pretrial confer-ence as part of early management | 0 | 0 | 0 | 0 |
| Effect of including joint discovery/ case management plan or status report as part of early management | 0 | 0 | 0 | 0 |
| Effect of including referral to mandatory arbitration as part of early management | 0 | 0 | 0 | 0 |
| Discovery: limiting interrogatories | 0 | 0 | 0 | 0 |
| Discovery: limiting depositions | NE | NE | NE | NE |
| Discovery: shortening time to cutoff | S − | S − | 0 | 0 |
| Mandatory early disclosure | 0 | 0 | S − district S + case | 0 |
| Voluntary early disclosure | 0 | 0 | 0 | 0 |
| Good-faith efforts before filing dis-covery motion | 0 | 0 | 0 | 0 |
| Litigants available at settlement conferences | S − | 0 | 0 | 0 |
| Increase use of magistrate judges to conduct civil pretrial case pro-cessing | 0 | 0 | S + | 0 |
| Track model of DCM | NE | NE | NE | NE |
| Complex case management | NE | NE | NE | NE |
| Party and lawyer sign continuance requests | NE | NE | NE | NE |
| Person with authority to bind at conferences | NE | NE | NE | NE |

S + = significant increase; 0 = no significant effect; S − = significant decrease; NE = not evaluated (see the text for reasons).

*A balanced package of policies could speed cases without affecting cost, satisfaction, or views of fairness.*

Our analysis of the effects of specific procedures and techniques suggests a package of case management policies with the potential to reduce time to disposition while not changing costs, satisfaction, and views of fairness. The package includes discovery control, the only case management practice that seemed to be effective in reducing costs:

*If early case management and early setting of a trial schedule are combined with shortened time to discovery cutoff, the increase in lawyer work hours predicted by early management can be offset by the decrease in lawyer work hours predicted by judicial control of discovery. We estimate that under these circumstances, litigants on general civil cases that do not close within the first nine months would pay no significant cost penalty for reduced time to disposition on the order of four to five months. None of these policies has any significant effect on lawyers' satisfaction or perceptions of fairness.*

Our analysis suggests that the following approach to early management of general civil litigation cases should be considered by courts and judges not currently using this approach and reemphasized by courts and judges that are using it. The powers to use this approach already exist under the Federal Rules of Civil Procedure.

- For cases that do not yet have issue joined, have a clerk monitor them to be sure deadlines for service and answer are met, and begin judicial action to dispose of the case if those deadlines are missed.

- For cases that have issue joined, wait a short time after the joinder date, perhaps a month, to see if the case terminates and then begin judicial case management.

- Include setting of a firm trial date as part of the early management package, and adhere to that date as much as possible.

- Include setting of a reasonably short discovery cutoff time tailored to the case as part of the early management package. For nearly all general civil cases, this policy should cause judicial case management to begin within six months or less after case filing.

# 8. IMPLEMENTING CHANGE

Given our understanding of how the civil justice system operates, we believe that this package of case management policies has a high probability of reducing time to disposition if implemented, without negatively affecting litigation costs or attorney views of satisfaction and fairness. However, our estimated effect should be treated as an upper bound to the effects that could be anticipated if the policies were implemented more widely.

*Our estimated effects of the case management package represent the upper bound of anticipated effects if the package is implemented widely.*

Our estimate is an upper bound rather than a precise estimate because our quantitative analyses used observational data on the naturally occurring variation in judges' management practices, rather than data resulting from an experimental random assignment of management practices to cases. We believe we have accurately estimated the effect of a given management practice among districts and judges who currently use it. However, any effects we observe must be interpreted in light of the constraints imposed by observational data.

In particular, judges and districts *choose* to use certain case management policies and practices, and we must assume that these judges and districts may differ from other judges and districts who choose *not* to use the same policies and practices. For example, judges who currently use early management may use it with greater intensity or effectiveness than other judges who may be asked to start using it in the future. Judges who use early management now might be using it in combination with other practices for which we do not have data (such as settlement discussion during the initial case management conference) and which other judges may not choose to use. Also, judges who do not use a particular case management practice now may continue not using it even if they are asked to start using it in the future.

Thus, successful use of a case management procedure by some judges in some districts does not necessarily mean it will be equally effective if all judges are asked to use the procedure in all districts. However, the limitations of observational data notwithstanding, practices that we have identified as effective among judges who currently use them are good candidates for practices that could be beneficial if more widely implemented.

The judiciary's ability to ensure widespread implementation of these promising practices is the key to achieving the positive effects we observe. Effective implementation of new policies can be enhanced by examining why the CJRA pilot program had little effect and by learning from prior court and organization research on implementation of change.

*Efforts to change the federal courts should accommodate the factors that impeded full implementation of the CJRA pilot program.*

Implementation factors that may have contributed to the pilot program's having little effect include: the vague wording of the act itself; the fact that some judges, lawyers, and others viewed the procedural innovations imposed by Congress as curtailing judicial independence accorded judges under Article III of the Constitution, and as unduly emphasizing speed and efficiency at the possible expense of justice; and the lack of effective mechanisms for ensuring that the policies contained in district plans were carried out on an ongoing basis.

Prior research on implementation indicates that change is not something "done to" members of an organization; rather, it is something they participate in, experience, and shape. Studies of change in the courts and in other organizations provide some guidelines for improving implementation. They include: clearly articulating what the change is to accomplish and generating a perceived need for it; a governance structure and process that coordinates individuals' activities and assigns accountability for results; and meaningful performance measures to help both implementers and overseers gauge progress.

Studies of change also document that members of organizations are more likely to change their behavior when leadership and commitment to change are embedded in the system, appropriate education is provided about what the change entails, relative performance is communicated across parts of the organization, all supporting elements in the organization also make desired changes, and sufficient resources are available.

Future efforts to change the federal civil justice system could be substantially enhanced by incorporating such guidelines.

# ICJ PUBLICATIONS

## OUTCOMES

### General

Carroll, S. J., with N. M. Pace, *Assessing the Effects of Tort Reforms*, R-3554-ICJ, 1987. $7.50.

Galanter, M., B. Garth, D. Hensler, and F. K. Zemans, *How to Improve Civil Justice Policy*, RP-282. (Reprinted from *Judicature*, Vol. 77, No. 4, January/February 1994.) Free.

Hensler, D. R., *Trends in California Tort Liability Litigation*, P-7287-ICJ, 1987. (Testimony before the Select Committee on Insurance, California State Assembly, October 1987.) $4.00.

_____ , *Researching Civil Justice: Problems and Pitfalls*, P-7604-ICJ, 1988. (Reprinted from *Law and Contemporary Problems*, Vol. 51, No. 3, Summer 1988.) $4.00.

_____ , *Reading the Tort Litigation Tea Leaves: What's Going on in the Civil Liability System?* RP-226. (Reprinted from *The Justice System Journal*, Vol. 16, No. 2, 1993.) Free.

_____ , *Why We Don't Know More About the Civil Justice System—and What We Could Do About It*, RP-363, 1995. (Reprinted from *USC Law*, Fall 1994.) Free.

Hensler, D. R., and E. Moller, *Trends in Punitive Damages: Preliminary Data from Cook County, Illinois, and San Francisco, California*, DRU-1014-ICJ, 1995. Free.

Hensler, D. R., M. E. Vaiana, J. S. Kakalik, and M. A. Peterson, *Trends in Tort Litigation: The Story Behind the Statistics*, R-3583-ICJ, 1987. $4.00.

Hill, P. T., and D. L. Madey, *Educational Policymaking Through the Civil Justice System*, R-2904-ICJ, 1982. $4.00.

Lipson, A. J., *California Enacts Prejudgment Interest: A Case Study of Legislative Action*, N-2096-ICJ, 1984. $4.00.

Moller, E., *Trends in Punitive Damages: Preliminary Data from California*, DRU-1059-ICJ, 1995. Free.

Shubert, G. H., *Some Observations on the Need for Tort Reform*, P-7189-ICJ, 1986. (Testimony before the National Conference of State Legislatures, January 1986.) $4.00.

_____ , *Changes in the Tort System: Helping Inform the Policy Debate*, P-7241-ICJ, 1986. $4.00.

### Jury Verdicts

Carroll, S. J., *Jury Awards and Prejudgment Interest in Tort Cases*, N-1994-ICJ, 1983. $4.00.

Chin, A., and M. A. Peterson, *Deep Pockets, Empty Pockets: Who Wins in Cook County Jury Trials*, R-3249-ICJ, 1985. $10.00.

Dertouzos, J. N., E. Holland, and P. A. Ebener, *The Legal and Economic Consequences of Wrongful Termination*, R-3602-ICJ, 1988. $7.50.

Hensler, D. R., *Summary of Research Results on the Tort Liability System*, P-7210-ICJ, 1986. (Testimony before the Committee on Commerce, Science, and Transportation, United States Senate, February 1986.) $4.00.

Hensler, D. R., and E. Moller, *Trends in Punitive Damages: Preliminary Data from Cook County, Illinois, and San Francisco, California*, DRU-1014-ICJ, 1995. Free.

MacCoun, R. J., *Getting Inside the Black Box: Toward a Better Understanding of Civil Jury Behavior*, N-2671-ICJ, 1987. $4.00.

_____ , *Experimental Research on Jury Decisionmaking*, R-3832-ICJ, 1989. (Reprinted from *Science*, Vol. 244, June 1989.) $4.00.

_____ , *Inside the Black Box: What Empirical Research Tells Us About Decisionmaking by Civil Juries*, RP-238, 1993. (Reprinted from Robert E. Litan, ed., *Verdict: Assessing the Civil Jury System*, The Brookings Institution, 1993.) Free.

_____ , *Is There a "Deep-Pocket" Bias in the Tort System?* IP-130, October 1993. Free.

_____ , *Blaming Others to a Fault?* RP-286. (Reprinted from *Chance*, Vol. 6, No. 4, Fall 1993.) Free.

_____ , *Improving Jury Comprehension in Criminal and Civil Trials*, CT-136, July 1995. Free.

Moller, E., *Trends in Punitive Damages: Preliminary Data from California*, DRU-1059-ICJ, 1995. Free.

_____ , *Trends in Civil Jury Verdicts Since 1985*, MR-694-ICJ, 1996. $15.00.

Peterson, M. A., *Compensation of Injuries: Civil Jury Verdicts in Cook County*, R-3011-ICJ, 1984. $7.50.

_____ , *Punitive Damages: Preliminary Empirical Findings*, N-2342-ICJ, 1985. $4.00.

_____ , *Summary of Research Results: Trends and Patterns in Civil Jury Verdicts*, P-7222-ICJ, 1986. (Testimony before the Subcommittee on Oversight, Committee on Ways and Means, United States House of Representatives, March 1986.) $4.00.

_____ , *Civil Juries in the 1980s: Trends in Jury Trials and Verdicts in California and Cook County, Illinois*, R-3466-ICJ, 1987. $7.50.

Peterson, M. A., and G. L. Priest, *The Civil Jury: Trends in Trials and Verdicts, Cook County, Illinois, 1960–1979*, R-2881-ICJ, 1982. $7.50.

Peterson, M. A., S. Sarma, and M. G. Shanley, *Punitive Damages: Empirical Findings*, R-3311-ICJ, 1987. $7.50.

Selvin, M., and L. Picus, *The Debate over Jury Performance: Observations from a Recent Asbestos Case*, R-3479-ICJ, 1987. $10.00.

Shanley, M. G., and M. A. Peterson, *Comparative Justice: Civil Jury Verdicts in San Francisco and Cook Counties, 1959–1980*, R-3006-ICJ, 1983. $7.50.

_____ , *Posttrial Adjustments to Jury Awards*, R-3511-ICJ, 1987. $7.50.

## Costs of Dispute Resolution

Dunworth, T., and J. S. Kakalik, *Preliminary Observations on Implementation of the Pilot Program of the Civil Justice Reform Act of 1990,* RP-361, 1995. (Reprinted from *Stanford Law Review,* Vol. 46, No. 6, July 1994.) Free.

Hensler, D. R., *Does ADR Really Save Money? The Jury's Still Out*, RP-327, 1994. (Reprinted from *The National Law Journal*, April 11, 1994.) Free.

Hensler, D. R., M. E. Vaiana, J. S. Kakalik, and M. A. Peterson, *Trends in Tort Litigation: The Story Behind the Statistics*, R-3583-ICJ, 1987. $4.00.

Kakalik, J. S., and A. E. Robyn, *Costs of the Civil Justice System: Court Expenditures for Processing Tort Cases*, R-2888-ICJ, 1982. $7.50.

Kakalik, J. S., and R. L. Ross, *Costs of the Civil Justice System: Court Expenditures for Various Types of Civil Cases*, R-2985-ICJ, 1983. $10.00.

Kakalik, J. S., P. A. Ebener, W. L. F. Felstiner, and M. G. Shanley, *Costs of Asbestos Litigation*, R-3042-ICJ, 1983. $4.00.

Kakalik, J. S., P. A. Ebener, W. L. F. Felstiner, G. W. Haggstrom, and M. G. Shanley, *Variation in Asbestos Litigation Compensation and Expenses*, R-3132-ICJ, 1984. $7.50.

Kakalik, J. S., and N. M. Pace, *Costs and Compensation Paid in Tort Litigation*, R-3391-ICJ, 1986. $15.00.

_____ , *Costs and Compensation Paid in Tort Litigation*, P-7243-ICJ, 1986. (Testimony before the Subcommittee on Trade, Productivity, and Economic Growth, Joint Economic Committee of the Congress, July 1986.) $4.00.

Kakalik, J. S., E. M. King, M. Traynor, P. A. Ebener, and L. Picus, *Costs and Compensation Paid in Aviation Accident Litigation*, R-3421-ICJ, 1988. $10.00.

Kakalik, J. S., M. Selvin, and N. M. Pace, *Averting Gridlock: Strategies for Reducing Civil Delay in the Los Angeles Superior Court*, R-3762-ICJ, 1990. $10.00.

Kakalik, J. S., T. Dunworth, L. A. Hill, D. McCaffrey, M. Oshiro, N. M. Pace, and M. E. Vaiana, *Just, Speedy, and Inexpensive? An Evaluation of Judicial Case Management Under the Civil Justice Reform Act*, MR-800-ICJ, 1996. $8.

Kakalik, J. S., T. Dunworth, L. A. Hill, D. McCaffrey, M. Oshiro, N. M. Pace, and M. E. Vaiana, *Implementation of the Civil Justice Reform Act in Pilot and Comparison Districts*, MR-801-ICJ, 1996. $20.

Kakalik, J. S., T. Dunworth, L. A. Hill, D. McCaffrey, M. Oshiro, N. M. Pace, and M. E. Vaiana, *An Evaluation of Judicial Case Management Under the Civil Justice Reform Act*, MR-802-ICJ, 1996. $20.

Kakalik, J. S., T. Dunworth, L. A. Hill, D. McCaffrey, M. Oshiro, N. M. Pace, and M. E. Vaiana, *An Evaluation of Mediation and Early Neutral Evaluation Under the Civil Justice Reform Act*, MR-803-ICJ, 1996. $20.

Lind, E. A., *Arbitrating High-Stakes Cases: An Evaluation of Court-Annexed Arbitration in a United States District Court*, R-3809-ICJ, 1990. $10.00.

MacCoun, R. J., E. A. Lind, D. R. Hensler, D. L. Bryant, and P. A. Ebener, *Alternative Adjudication: An Evaluation of the New Jersey Automobile Arbitration Program*, R-3676-ICJ, 1988. $10.00.

Peterson, M. A., *New Tools for Reducing Civil Litigation Expenses*, R-3013-ICJ, 1983. $4.00.

Priest, G. L., *Regulating the Content and Volume of Litigation: An Economic Analysis*, R-3084-ICJ, 1983. $4.00.

## DISPUTE RESOLUTION

### Court Delay

Adler, J. W., W. L. F. Felstiner, D. R. Hensler, and M. A. Peterson, *The Pace of Litigation: Conference Proceedings*, R-2922-ICJ, 1982. $10.00.

Dunworth, T., and J. S. Kakalik, *Preliminary Observations on Implementation of the Pilot Program of the Civil Justice Reform Act of 1990*, RP-361, 1995. (Reprinted from *Stanford Law Review*, Vol. 46, No. 6, July 1994.) Free.

Dunworth, T., and N. M. Pace, *Statistical Overview of Civil Litigation in the Federal Courts*, R-3885-ICJ, 1990. $7.50.

Ebener, P. A., *Court Efforts to Reduce Pretrial Delay: A National Inventory*, R-2732-ICJ, 1981. $10.00.

Kakalik, J. S., M. Selvin, and N. M. Pace, *Averting Gridlock: Strategies for Reducing Civil Delay in the Los Angeles Superior Court*, R-3762-ICJ, 1990. $10.00.

_____ , *Strategies for Reducing Civil Delay in the Los Angeles Superior Court: Technical Appendixes*, N-2988-ICJ, 1990. $10.00.

Kakalik, J. S., T. Dunworth, L. A. Hill, D. McCaffrey, M. Oshiro, N. M. Pace, and M. E. Vaiana, *Just, Speedy, and Inexpensive? An Evaluation of Judicial Case Management Under the Civil Justice Reform Act*, MR-800-ICJ, 1996. $8.

Kakalik, J. S., T. Dunworth, L. A. Hill, D. McCaffrey, M. Oshiro, N. M. Pace, and M. E. Vaiana, *Implementation of the Civil Justice Reform Act in Pilot and Comparison Districts*, MR-801-ICJ, 1996. $20.

Kakalik, J. S., T. Dunworth, L. A. Hill, D. McCaffrey, M. Oshiro, N. M. Pace, and M. E. Vaiana, *An Evaluation of Judicial Case Management Under the Civil Justice Reform Act*, MR-802-ICJ, 1996. $20.

Kakalik, J. S., T. Dunworth, L. A. Hill, D. McCaffrey, M. Oshiro, N. M. Pace, and M. E. Vaiana, *An Evaluation of Mediation and Early Neutral Evaluation Under the Civil Justice Reform Act*, MR-803-ICJ, 1996. $20.

Lind, E. A., *Arbitrating High-Stakes Cases: An Evaluation of Court-Annexed Arbitration in a United States District Court*, R-3809-ICJ, 1990. $10.00.

MacCoun, R. J., E. A. Lind, D. R. Hensler, D. L. Bryant, and P. A. Ebener, *Alternative Adjudication: An Evaluation of the New Jersey Automobile Arbitration Program*, R-3676-ICJ, 1988. $10.00.

Resnik, J., *Managerial Judges*, R-3002-ICJ, 1982. (Reprinted from the *Harvard Law Review*, Vol. 96:374, December 1982.) $7.50.

Selvin, M., and P. A. Ebener, *Managing the Unmanageable: A History of Civil Delay in the Los Angeles Superior Court*, R-3165-ICJ, 1984. $15.00.

## Alternative Dispute Resolution

Adler, J. W., D. R. Hensler, and C. E. Nelson, with the assistance of G. J. Rest, *Simple Justice: How Litigants Fare in the Pittsburgh Court Arbitration Program*, R-3071-ICJ, 1983. $15.00.

Bryant, D. L., *Judicial Arbitration in California: An Update*, N-2909-ICJ, 1989. $4.00.

Ebener, P. A., and D. R. Betancourt, *Court-Annexed Arbitration: The National Picture*, N-2257-ICJ, 1985. $25.00.

Hensler, D. R., *Court-Annexed Arbitration in the State Trial Court System*, P-6963-ICJ, 1984. (Testimony before the Judiciary Committee Subcommittee on Courts, United States Senate, February 1984.) $4.00.

_____ , *Reforming the Civil Litigation Process: How Court Arbitration Can Help*, P-7027-ICJ, 1984. (Reprinted from the *New Jersey Bell Journal*, August 1984.) $4.00.

_____ , *What We Know and Don't Know About Court-Administered Arbitration*, N-2444-ICJ, 1986. $4.00.

_____ , *Court-Ordered Arbitration: An Alternative View*, RP-103, 1992. (Reprinted from *The University of Chicago Legal Forum*, Vol. 1990.) Free.

_____ , *Science in the Court: Is There a Role for Alternative Dispute Resolution?* RP-109, 1992. (Reprinted from *Law and Contemporary Problems*, Vol. 54, No. 3, Summer 1991.) Free.

_____ , *Does ADR Really Save Money? The Jury's Still Out*, RP-327, 1994. (Reprinted from *The National Law Journal*, April 11, 1994.) Free.

_____ , *A Glass Half Full, a Glass Half Empty: The Use of Alternative Dispute Resolution in Mass Personal Injury Litigation*, RP-446, 1995. (Reprinted from *Texas Law Review*, Vol. 73, No. 7, June 1995.) Free.

Hensler, D. R., A. J. Lipson, and E. S. Rolph, *Judicial Arbitration in California: The First Year*, R-2733-ICJ, 1981. $10.00.

_____ , *Judicial Arbitration in California: The First Year: Executive Summary*, R-2733/1-ICJ, 1981. $4.00.

Hensler, D. R., and J. W. Adler, with the assistance of G. J. Rest, *Court-Administered Arbitration: An Alternative for Consumer Dispute Resolution*, N-1965-ICJ, 1983. $4.00.

Kakalik, J. S., T. Dunworth, L. A. Hill, D. McCaffrey, M. Oshiro, N. M. Pace, and M. E. Vaiana, *An Evaluation of Mediation and Early Neutral Evaluation Under the Civil Justice Reform Act*, MR-803-ICJ, 1996. $20.

Lind, E. A., *Arbitrating High-Stakes Cases: An Evaluation of Court-Annexed Arbitration in a United States District Court*, R-3809-ICJ, 1990. $10.00.

Lind, E. A., R. J. MacCoun, P. A. Ebener, W. L. F. Felstiner, D. R. Hensler, J. Resnik, and T. R. Tyler, *The Perception of Justice: Tort Litigants' Views of Trial, Court-Annexed Arbitration, and Judicial Settlement Conferences*, R-3708-ICJ, 1989. $7.50.

MacCoun, R. J., *Unintended Consequences of Court Arbitration: A Cautionary Tale from New Jersey*, RP-134, 1992. (Reprinted from *The Justice System Journal*, Vol. 14, No. 2, 1991.) Free.

MacCoun, R. J., E. A. Lind, D. R. Hensler, D. L. Bryant, and P. A. Ebener, *Alternative Adjudication: An Evaluation of the New Jersey Automobile Arbitration Program*, R-3676-ICJ, 1988. $10.00.

MacCoun, R. J., E. A. Lind, and T. R. Tyler, *Alternative Dispute Resolution in Trial and Appellate Courts*, RP-117, 1992. (Reprinted from *Handbook of Psychology and Law*, 1992.) Free.

Moller, E., E. S. Rolph, P. Ebener, *Private Dispute Resolution in the Banking Industry*, MR-259-ICJ, 1993. $13.00.

Resnik, J. *Many Doors? Closing Doors? Alternative Dispute Resolution and Adjudication*, RP-439, 1995. (Reprinted from The Ohio State Journal on Dispute Resolution, Vol. 10, No. 2, 1995.) Free.

Rolph, E. S., *Introducing Court-Annexed Arbitration: A Policymaker's Guide*, R-3167-ICJ, 1984. $10.00.

Rolph, E. S., and D. R. Hensler, *Court-Ordered Arbitration: The California Experience*, N-2186-ICJ, 1984. $4.00.

Rolph, E. S., and E. Moller, *Evaluating Agency Alternative Dispute Resolution Programs: A Users' Guide to Data Collection and Use*, MR-534-ACUS/ICJ, 1995. $13.00.

Rolph, E. S., E. Moller, and L. Petersen, *Escaping the Courthouse: Private Alternative Dispute Resolution in Los Angeles*, MR-472-JRHD/ICJ, 1994. $15.00.

## Special Issues

Kritzer, H. M., W. L. F. Felstiner, A. Sarat, and D. M. Trubek, *The Impact of Fee Arrangement on Lawyer Effort*, P-7180-ICJ, 1986. $4.00.

Priest, G. L., *Regulating the Content and Volume of Litigation: An Economic Analysis*, R-3084-ICJ, 1983. $4.00.

Priest, G. L., and B. Klein, *The Selection of Disputes for Litigation*, R-3032-ICJ, 1984. $7.50.

Resnik, J., *Managerial Judges*, R-3002-ICJ, 1982. (Reprinted from the *Harvard Law Review*, Vol. 96:374, December 1982.) $7.50.

_____ , *Failing Faith: Adjudicatory Procedure in Decline*, P-7272-ICJ, 1987. (Reprinted from the *University of Chicago Law Review*, Vol. 53, No. 2, 1986.) $7.50.

_____ , *Due Process: A Public Dimension*, P-7418-ICJ, 1988. (Reprinted from the *University of Florida Law Review*, Vol. 39, No. 2, 1987.) $4.00.

_____ , *Judging Consent*, P-7419-ICJ, 1988. (Reprinted from the *University of Chicago Legal Forum*, Vol. 1987.) $7.50.

_____ , *From "Cases" to "Litigation,"* RP-110, 1992. (Reprinted from *Law and Contemporary Problems*, Vol. 54, No. 3, Summer 1991.) Free.

_____ , *Whose Judgment? Vacating Judgments, Preferences for Settlement, and the Role of Adjudication at the Close of the Twentieth Century*, RP-364, 1995. (Reprinted from *UCLA Law Review*, Vol. 41, No. 6, August 1994.) Free.

## AREAS OF LIABILITY

### Auto-Accident Litigation

Abrahamse, A., and S. J. Carroll, *The Effects of a Choice Auto Insurance Plan on Insurance Costs*, MR-540-ICJ, 1995. $13.00.

———, *The Effects of Proposition 213 on the Costs of Auto Insurance in California*, IP-157, September 1996. Free.

Carroll, S. J., and A. Abrahamse, *The Effects of a Proposed No-Fault Plan on the Costs of Auto Insurance in California*, IP-146, March 1995. Free.

———, *The Effects of a Proposed No-Fault Plan on the Costs of Auto Insurance in California: An Updated Analysis*, January 1996. Free.

Carroll, S. J., and J. S. Kakalik, *No-Fault Approaches to Compensating Auto Accident Victims*, RP-229, 1993. (Reprinted from *The Journal of Risk and Insurance*, Vol. 60, No. 2, 1993.) Free.

Carroll, S. J., A. Abrahamse, and M. E. Vaiana, *The Costs of Excess Medical Claims for Automobile Personal Injuries*, DB-139-ICJ, 1995. $6.00.

Carroll, S. J., J. S. Kakalik, N. M. Pace, and J. L. Adams, *No-Fault Approaches to Compensating People Injured in Automobile Accidents*, R-4019-ICJ, 1991. $20.00.

Carroll, S. J., and J. S. Kakalik, with D. Adamson, *No-Fault Automobile Insurance: A Policy Perspective*, R-4019/1-ICJ, 1991. $4.00.

Hammitt, J. K., *Automobile Accident Compensation, Volume II, Payments by Auto Insurers*, R-3051-ICJ, 1985. $10.00.

Hammitt, J. K., and J. E. Rolph, *Limiting Liability for Automobile Accidents: Are No-Fault Tort Thresholds Effective?* N-2418-ICJ, 1985. $4.00.

Hammitt, J. K., R. L. Houchens, S. S. Polin, and J. E. Rolph, *Automobile Accident Compensation: Volume IV, State Rules*, R-3053-ICJ, 1985. $7.50.

Houchens, R. L., *Automobile Accident Compensation: Volume III, Payments from All Sources*, R-3052-ICJ, 1985. $7.50.

MacCoun, R. J., E. A. Lind, D. R. Hensler, D. L. Bryant, and P. A. Ebener, *Alternative Adjudication: An Evaluation of the New Jersey Automobile Arbitration Program*, R-3676-ICJ, 1988. $10.00.

O'Connell, J., S. J. Carroll, M. Horowitz, and A. Abrahamse, *Consumer Choice in the Auto Insurance Market*, RP-254, 1994. (Reprinted from the *Maryland Law Review*, Vol. 52, 1993.) Free.

O'Connell, J., S. J. Carroll, M. Horowitz, A. Abrahamse, and D. Kaiser, *The Costs of Consumer Choice for Auto Insurance in States Without No-Fault Insurance*, RP-442, 1995. (Reprinted from *Maryland Law Review*, Vol. 54, No. 2, 1995.) Free.

Rolph, J. E., with J. K. Hammitt, R. L. Houchens, and S. S. Polin, *Automobile Accident Compensation: Volume I, Who Pays How Much How Soon?* R-3050-ICJ, 1985. $4.00.

## Asbestos

Hensler, D. R., *Resolving Mass Toxic Torts: Myths and Realities*, P-7631-ICJ, 1990. (Reprinted from the *University of Illinois Law Review*, Vol. 1989, No. 1.) $4.00.

_____ , *Asbestos Litigation in the United States: A Brief Overview*, P-7776-ICJ, 1992. (Testimony before the Courts and Judicial Administration Subcommittee, United States House Judiciary Committee, October 1991.) $4.00.

_____ , *Assessing Claims Resolution Facilities: What We Need to Know*, RP-107, 1992. (Reprinted from *Law and Contemporary Problems*, Vol. 53, No. 4, Autumn 1990.) Free.

_____ , *Fashioning a National Resolution of Asbestos Personal Injury Litigation: A Reply to Professor Brickman*, RP-114, 1992. (Reprinted from *Cardozo Law Review*, Vol. 13, No. 6, April 1992.) Free.

Hensler, D. R., W. L. F. Felstiner, M. Selvin, and P. A. Ebener, *Asbestos in the Courts: The Challenge of Mass Toxic Torts*, R-3324-ICJ, 1985. $10.00.

Kakalik, J. S., P. A. Ebener, W. L. F. Felstiner, and M. G. Shanley, *Costs of Asbestos Litigation*, R-3042-ICJ, 1983. $4.00.

Kakalik, J. S., P. A. Ebener, W. L. F. Felstiner, G. W. Haggstrom, and M. G. Shanley, *Variation in Asbestos Litigation Compensation and Expenses*, R-3132-ICJ, 1984. $7.50.

Peterson, M. A., *Giving Away Money: Comparative Comments on Claims Resolution Facilities*, RP-108, 1992. (Reprinted from *Law and Contemporary Problems*, Vol. 53, No. 4, Autumn 1990.) Free.

Peterson, M. A., and M. Selvin, *Resolution of Mass Torts: Toward a Framework for Evaluation of Aggregative Procedures*, N-2805-ICJ, 1988. $7.50.

_____ , *Mass Justice: The Limited and Unlimited Power of Courts*, RP-116, 1992. (Reprinted from *Law and Contemporary Problems*, No. 3, Summer 1991.) Free.

Selvin, M., and L. Picus, *The Debate over Jury Performance: Observations from a Recent Asbestos Case*, R-3479-ICJ, 1987. $10.00.

## Aviation Accidents

Kakalik, J. S., E. M. King, M. Traynor, P. A. Ebener, and L. Picus, *Costs and Compensation Paid in Aviation Accident Litigation*, R-3421-ICJ, 1988. $10.00.

_____ , *Aviation Accident Litigation Survey: Data Collection Forms*, N-2773-ICJ, 1988. $7.50.

King, E. M., and J. P. Smith, *Computing Economic Loss in Cases of Wrongful Death*, R-3549-ICJ, 1988. $10.00.

_____ , *Economic Loss and Compensation in Aviation Accidents*, R-3551-ICJ, 1988. $10.00.

_____ , *Dispute Resolution Following Airplane Crashes*, R-3585-ICJ, 1988. $7.50.

*Executive Summaries of the Aviation Accident Study*, R-3684, 1988. $7.50.

## Employment

Dertouzos, J. N., E. Holland, and P. A. Ebener, *The Legal and Economic Consequences of Wrongful Termination*, R-3602-ICJ, 1988. $7.50.

Dertouzos, J. N., and L. A. Karoly, *Labor-Market Responses to Employer Liability*, R-3989-ICJ, 1992. $7.50.

## Environment: California's Clean-Air Strategy

Dixon, L. S., and S. Garber, *California's Ozone-Reduction Strategy for Light-Duty Vehicles: Direct Costs, Direct Emission Effects and Market Responses*, MR-695-ICJ, 1996. $13.00.

————, *Economic Perspectives on Revising California's Zero-Emission Vehicle Mandate*, CT-137, March 1996. $5.00.

Dixon, L. S., S. Garber, and M. E. Vaiana, *California's Ozone-Reduction Strategy for Light-Duty Vehicles: An Economic Assessment*, MR-695/1-ICJ, 1996. $15.00.

————, *Making ZEV Policy Despite Uncertainty: An Annotated Briefing for the California Air Resources Board*, DRU-1266-1-ICJ, 1995. Free.

## Environment: Superfund

Acton, J. P., *Understanding Superfund: A Progress Report*, R-3838-ICJ, 1989. $7.50.

Acton, J. P., and L. S. Dixon with D. Drezner, L. Hill, and S. McKenney, *Superfund and Transaction Costs: The Experiences of Insurers and Very Large Industrial Firms*, R-4132-ICJ, 1992. $7.50.

Dixon, L. S., *RAND Research on Superfund Transaction Costs: A Summary of Findings to Date*, CT-111, November 1993. $5.00.

————, *Fixing Superfund: The Effect of the Proposed Superfund Reform Act of 1994 on Transaction Costs*, MR-455-ICJ, 1994. $15.00.

————, *Superfund Liability Reform: Implications for Transaction Costs and Site Cleanup*, CT-125, 1995. $5.00.

Dixon, L. S., D. S. Drezner, and J. K. Hammitt, *Private-Sector Cleanup Expenditures and Transaction Costs at 18 Superfund Sites*, MR-204-EPA/RC, 1993. $13.00.

Reuter, P., *The Economic Consequences of Expanded Corporate Liability: An Exploratory Study*, N-2807-ICJ, 1988. $7.50.

## Medical Malpractice

Danzon, P. M., *Contingent Fees for Personal Injury Litigation*, R-2458-HCFA, 1980. $4.00.

————, *The Disposition of Medical Malpractice Claims*, R-2622-HCFA, 1980. $7.50.

————, *Why Are Malpractice Premiums So High—Or So Low?* R-2623-HCFA, 1980. $4.00.

————, *The Frequency and Severity of Medical Malpractice Claims*, R-2870-ICJ/HCFA, 1982. $7.50.

————, *New Evidence on the Frequency and Severity of Medical Malpractice Claims*, R-3410-ICJ, 1986. $4.00.

_____ , *The Effects of Tort Reform on the Frequency and Severity of Medical Malpractice Claims: A Summary of Research Results*, P-7211, 1986. (Testimony before the Committee on the Judiciary, United States Senate, March 1986.) $4.00.

Danzon, P. M., and L. A. Lillard, *The Resolution of Medical Malpractice Claims: Modeling the Bargaining Process*, R-2792-ICJ, 1982. $7.50.

_____ , *Settlement Out of Court: The Disposition of Medical Malpractice Claims*, P-6800, 1982. $4.00.

_____ , *The Resolution of Medical Malpractice Claims: Research Results and Policy Implications*, R-2793-ICJ, 1982. $4.00.

Kravitz, R. L. , J. E. Rolph, K. A. McGuigan, *Malpractice Claims Data as a Quality Improvement Tool: I. Epidemiology of Error in Four Specialties*, N-3448/1-RWJ, 1991. $4.00.

Lewis, E., and J. E. Rolph, *The Bad Apples? Malpractice Claims Experience of Physicians with a Surplus Lines Insurer*, P-7812, 1993. $4.00.

Rolph, E. S., *Health Care Delivery and Tort: Systems on a Collision Course?* Conference Proceedings, Dallas, June 1991, N-3524-ICJ, 1992. $10.00.

Rolph, J. E., *Some Statistical Evidence on Merit Rating in Medical Malpractice Insurance*, N-1725-HHS, 1981. $4.00.

_____ , *Merit Rating for Physicians' Malpractice Premiums: Only a Modest Deterrent*, N-3426-MT/RWJ/RC, 1991. $4.00.

Rolph, J. E., R. L. Kravitz, and K. A. McGuigan, *Malpractice Claims Data as a Quality Improvement Tool: II. Is Targeting Effective?* N-3448/2-RWJ, 1991. $4.00.

Williams, A. P., *Malpractice, Outcomes, and Appropriateness of Care*, P-7445, May 1988. $4.00.

## Product Liability

Dunworth, T., *Product Liability and the Business Sector: Litigation Trends in Federal Courts*, R-3668-ICJ, 1988. $7.50.

Eads, G., and P. Reuter, *Designing Safer Products: Corporate Responses to Product Liability Law and Regulation*, R-3022-ICJ, 1983. $15.00.

_____ , *Designing Safer Products: Corporate Responses to Product Liability Law and Regulation*, P-7089-ICJ, 1985. (Reprinted from the *Journal of Product Liability*, Vol. 7, 1985.) $4.00.

Garber, S., *Product Liability and the Economics of Pharmaceuticals and Medical Devices*, R-4285-ICJ, 1993. $15.00.

Hensler, D. R., *Summary of Research Results on Product Liability*, P-7271-ICJ, 1986. (Statement submitted to the Committee on the Judiciary, United States Senate, October 1986.) $4.00.

_____ , *What We Know and Don't Know About Product Liability*, P-7775-ICJ, 1993. (Statement submitted to the Commerce Committee, United States Senate, September 1991.) $4.00.

Moller, E., *Trends in Civil Jury Verdicts Since 1985*, MR-694-ICJ, 1996. $15.00.

Peterson, M. A., *Civil Juries in the 1980s: Trends in Jury Trials and Verdicts in California and Cook County, Illinois*, R-3466-ICJ, 1987. $7.50.

Reuter, P., *The Economic Consequences of Expanded Corporate Liability: An Exploratory Study*, N-2807-ICJ, 1988. $7.50.

**Workers' Compensation**

Darling-Hammond, L., and T. J. Kniesner, *The Law and Economics of Workers' Compensation*, R-2716-ICJ, 1980. $7.50.

Victor, R. B., *Workers' Compensation and Workplace Safety: The Nature of Employer Financial Incentives*, R-2979-ICJ, 1982. $7.50.

Victor, R. B., L. R. Cohen, and C. E. Phelps, *Workers' Compensation and Workplace Safety: Some Lessons from Economic Theory*, R-2918-ICJ, 1982. $7.50.

## MASS TORTS AND CLASS ACTIONS

Hensler, D. R., *Resolving Mass Toxic Torts: Myths and Realities*, P-7631-ICJ, 1990. (Reprinted from the *University of Illinois Law Review*, Vol. 1989, No. 1.) $4.00.

_____ , *Asbestos Litigation in the United States: A Brief Overview*, P-7776-ICJ, 1992. (Testimony before the Courts and Judicial Administration Subcommittee, United States House Judiciary Committee, October 1991.) $4.00.

_____ , *Assessing Claims Resolution Facilities: What We Need to Know*, RP-107, 1992. (Reprinted from *Law and Contemporary Problems*, Vol. 53, No. 4, Autumn 1990.) Free.

_____ , *Fashioning a National Resolution of Asbestos Personal Injury Litigation: A Reply to Professor Brickman*, RP-114, 1992. (Reprinted from *Cardozo Law Review*, Vol. 13, No. 6, April 1992.) Free.

Hensler, D. R., W. L. F. Felstiner, M. Selvin, and P. A. Ebener, *Asbestos in the Courts: The Challenge of Mass Toxic Torts*, R-3324-ICJ, 1985. $10.00.

Hensler, D. R., M. A. Peterson, *Understanding Mass Personal Injury Litigation: A Socio-Legal Analysis*, RP-311, 1994. (Reprinted from *Brooklyn Law Review*, Vol. 59, No. 3, Fall 1993.) Free.

Kakalik, J. S., P. A. Ebener, W. L. F. Felstiner, G. W. Haggstrom, and M. G. Shanley, *Variation in Asbestos Litigation Compensation and Expenses*, R-3132-ICJ, 1984. $7.50.

Kakalik, J. S., P. A. Ebener, W. L. F. Felstiner, and M. G. Shanley, *Costs of Asbestos Litigation*, R-3042-ICJ, 1983. $4.00.

Peterson, M. A., *Giving Away Money: Comparative Comments on Claims Resolution Facilities*, RP-108, 1992. (Reprinted from *Law and Contemporary Problems*, Vol. 53, No. 4, Autumn 1990.) Free.

Peterson, M. A., and M. Selvin, *Resolution of Mass Torts: Toward a Framework for Evaluation of Aggregative Procedures*, N-2805-ICJ, 1988. $7.50.

_____ , *Mass Justice: The Limited and Unlimited Power of Courts*, RP-116, 1992. (Reprinted from *Law and Contemporary Problems*, Vol. 54, No. 3, Summer 1991.) Free.

Selvin, M., and L. Picus, *The Debate over Jury Performance: Observations from a Recent Asbestos Case*, R-3479-ICJ, 1987. $10.00.

Dixon, L. S., D. S. Drezner, and J. K. Hammitt, *Private-Sector Cleanup Expenditures and Transaction Costs at 18 Superfund Sites*, MR-204-EPA/RC, 1993. $13.00.

## TRENDS IN THE TORT LITIGATION SYSTEM

Galanter, M., B. Garth, D. Hensler, and F. K. Zemans, *How to Improve Civil Justice Policy*, RP-282. (Reprinted from *Judicature*, Vol. 77, No. 4, January/February 1994.) Free.

Hensler, D. R., *Trends in California Tort Liability Litigation*, P-7287-ICJ, 1987. (Testimony before the Select Committee on Insurance, California State Assembly, October 1987.) $4.00.

_____ , *Reading the Tort Litigation Tea Leaves: What's Going on in the Civil Liability System?* RP-226. (Reprinted from *The Justice System Journal*, Vol. 16, No. 2, 1993.) Free.

Hensler, D. R., M. E. Vaiana, J. S. Kakalik, and M. A. Peterson, *Trends in Tort Litigation: The Story Behind the Statistics*, R-3583-ICJ, 1987. $4.00.

## ECONOMIC EFFECTS OF THE LIABILITY SYSTEM

### General

Carroll, S. J., A. Abrahamse, M. S. Marquis, and M. E. Vaiana, *Liability System Incentives to Consume Excess Medical Care*, DRU-1264-ICJ, 1995. Free.

Johnson, L. L., *Cost-Benefit Analysis and Voluntary Safety Standards for Consumer Products*, R-2882-ICJ, 1982. $7.50.

Reuter, P., *The Economic Consequences of Expanded Corporate Liability: An Exploratory Study*, N-2807-ICJ, 1988. $7.50.

### Product Liability

Dunworth, T., *Product Liability and the Business Sector: Litigation Trends in Federal Courts*, R-3668-ICJ, 1988. $7.50.

Eads, G., and P. Reuter, *Designing Safer Products: Corporate Responses to Product Liability Law and Regulation*, R-3022-ICJ, 1983. $15.00.

_____ , *Designing Safer Products: Corporate Responses to Product Liability Law and Regulation*, P-7089-ICJ, 1985. (Reprinted from the *Journal of Product Liability*, Vol. 7, 1985.) $4.00.

Garber, S., *Product Liability and the Economics of Pharmaceuticals and Medical Devices*, R-4285-ICJ, 1993. $15.00.

Hensler, D. R., *Summary of Research Results on Product Liability*, P-7271-ICJ, 1986. (Statement submitted to the Committee on the Judiciary, United States Senate, October 1986.) $4.00.

_____ , *What We Know and Don't Know About Product Liability*, P-7775-ICJ, 1993. (Statement submitted to the Commerce Committee, United States Senate, September 1991.) $4.00.

Peterson, M. A., *Civil Juries in the 1980s: Trends in Jury Trials and Verdicts in California and Cook County, Illinois*, R-3466-ICJ, 1987. $7.50.

## Wrongful Termination

Dertouzos, J. N., E. Holland, and P. A. Ebener, *The Legal and Economic Consequences of Wrongful Termination*, R-3602-ICJ, 1988. $7.50.

Dertouzos, J. N., and L. A. Karoly, *Labor-Market Responses to Employer Liability*, R-3989-ICJ, 1992. $7.50.

# COMPENSATION SYSTEMS

## System Design

Darling-Hammond, L., and T. J. Kniesner, *The Law and Economics of Workers' Compensation*, R-2716-ICJ, 1980. $7.50.

Hammitt, J. K., R. L. Houchens, S. S. Polin, and J. E. Rolph, *Automobile Accident Compensation: Volume IV, State Rules*, R-3053-ICJ, 1985. $7.50.

Hammitt, J. K., and J. E. Rolph, *Limiting Liability for Automobile Accidents: Are No-Fault Tort Thresholds Effective?* N-2418-ICJ, 1985. $4.00.

Hensler, D. R., *Resolving Mass Toxic Torts: Myths and Realities*, P-7631-ICJ, 1990. (Reprinted from the *University of Illinois Law Review*, Vol. 1989, No. 1.) $4.00.

_____ , *Assessing Claims Resolution Facilities: What We Need to Know*, RP-107, 1992. (Reprinted from *Law and Contemporary Problems*, Vol. 53, No. 4, Autumn 1990.) Free.

King, E. M., and J. P. Smith, *Computing Economic Loss in Cases of Wrongful Death*, R-3549-ICJ, 1988. $10.00.

Peterson, M. A., and M. Selvin, *Resolution of Mass Torts: Toward a Framework for Evaluation of Aggregative Procedures*, N-2805-ICJ, 1988. $7.50.

Rolph, E. S., *Framing the Compensation Inquiry*, RP-115, 1992. (Reprinted from the *Cardozo Law Review*, Vol. 13, No. 6, April 1992.) Free.

Victor, R. B., *Workers' Compensation and Workplace Safety: The Nature of Employer Financial Incentives*, R-2979-ICJ, 1982. $7.50.

Victor, R. B., L. R. Cohen, and C. E. Phelps, *Workers' Compensation and Workplace Safety: Some Lessons from Economic Theory*, R-2918-ICJ, 1982. $7.50.

## Performance

Abrahamse, A., and S. J. Carroll, *The Effects of a Choice Auto Insurance Plan on Insurance Costs*, MR-540-ICJ, 1995. $13.00.

Carroll, S. J., and A. Abrahamse, *The Effects of a Proposed No-Fault Plan on the Costs of Auto Insurance in California*, IP-146, March 1995. Free.

Carroll, S. J., and J. S. Kakalik, *No-Fault Approaches to Compensating Auto Accident Victims*, RP-229, 1993. (Reprinted from *The Journal of Risk and Insurance*, Vol. 60, No. 2, 1993.) Free.

Carroll, S. J., A. Abrahamse, and M. E. Vaiana, *The Costs of Excess Medical Claims for Automobile Personal Injuries*, DB-139-ICJ, 1995. $6.00.

Carroll, S. J., A. Abrahamse, M. S. Marquis, and M. E. Vaiana, *Liability System Incentives to Consume Excess Medical Care*, DRU-1264-ICJ, 1995. Free.

Carroll, S. J., J. S. Kakalik, N. M. Pace, and J. L. Adams, *No-Fault Approaches to Compensating People Injured in Automobile Accidents*, R-4019-ICJ, 1991. $20.00.

Carroll, S. J., and J. S. Kakalik, with D. Adamson, *No-Fault Automobile Insurance: A Policy Perspective*, R-4019/1-ICJ, 1991. $4.00.

Hensler, D. R., M. S. Marquis, A. Abrahamse, S. H. Berry, P. A. Ebener, E. G. Lewis, E. A. Lind, R. J. MacCoun, W. G. Manning, J. A. Rogowski, and M. E. Vaiana, *Compensation for Accidental Injuries in the United States*, R-3999-HHS/ICJ, 1991. $20.00.

_____ , *Compensation for Accidental Injuries in the United States: Executive Summary*, R-3999/1-HHS/ICJ, 1991. $4.00.

_____ , *Compensation for Accidental Injuries: Research Design and Methods*, N-3230-HHS/ICJ, 1991. $15.00.

King, E. M., and J. P. Smith, *Economic Loss and Compensation in Aviation Accidents*, R-3551-ICJ, 1988. $10.00.

O'Connell, J., S. J. Carroll, M. Horowitz, and A. Abrahamse, *Consumer Choice in the Auto Insurance Market*, RP-254, 1994. (Reprinted from the *Maryland Law Review*, Vol. 52, 1993.) Free.

O'Connell, J., S. J. Carroll, M. Horowitz, A. Abrahamse, and D. Kaiser, *The Costs of Consumer Choice for Auto Insurance in States Without No-Fault Insurance*, RP-442, 1995. (Reprinted from *Maryland Law Review*, Vol. 54, No. 2, 1995.) Free.

Peterson, M. A., *Giving Away Money: Comparative Comments on Claims Resolution Facilities*, RP-108, 1992. (Reprinted from *Law and Contemporary Problems*, Vol. 53, No. 4, Autumn 1990.) Free.

Peterson, M. A., and M. Selvin, *Mass Justice: The Limited and Unlimited Power of Courts*, RP-116, 1992. (Reprinted from *Law and Contemporary Problems*, Vol. 54, No. 3, Summer 1991.) Free.

Rolph, J. E., with J. K. Hammitt, R. L. Houchens, and S. S. Polin, *Automobile Accident Compensation: Volume I, Who Pays How Much How Soon?* R-3050-ICJ, 1985. $4.00.

## SPECIAL STUDIES

Hensler, D. R., and M. E. Reddy, *California Lawyers View the Future: A Report to the Commission on the Future of the Legal Profession and the State Bar*, MR-528-ICJ, 1994. $13.00.

Merz, J. F., and N. M. Pace, *Trends in Patent Litigation: The Apparent Influence of Strengthened Patents Attributable to the Court of Appeals for the Federal Circuit*, RP-426, 1995. (Reprinted from *Journal of the Patent and Trademark Office Society*, Vol. 76, No. 8, August 1994.) Free.

An annotated bibliography, CP-253 (12/96), provides a list of RAND publications in the civil justice area through 1996 To request the bibliography or to obtain more information about the Institute for Civil Justice, please write the Institute at this address: The Institute for Civil Justice, RAND, 1700 Main Street, P.O. Box 2138, Santa Monica, California 90407-2138, or call (310) 393-0411, x6916.